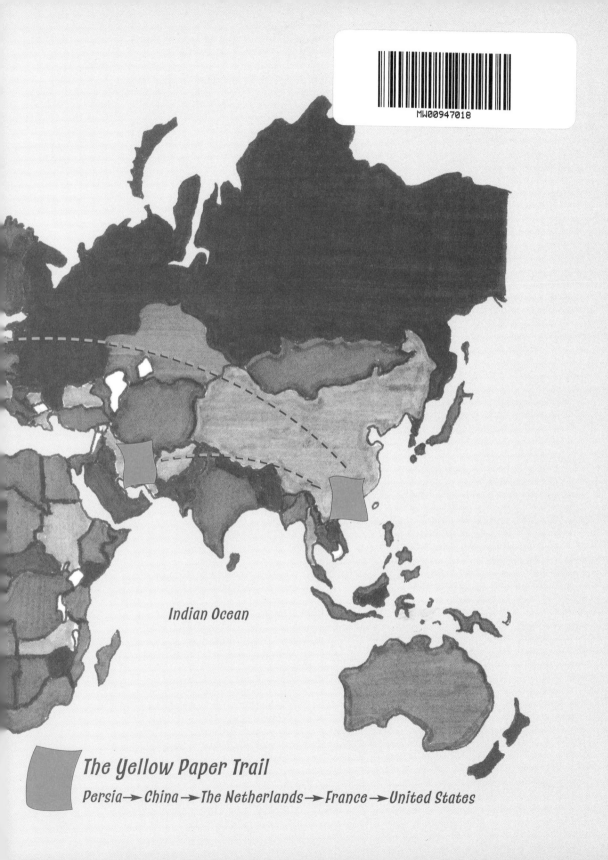

MW00947018

Indian Ocean

The Yellow Paper Trail

Persia ➤ China ➤ The Netherlands ➤ France ➤ United States

BRIGHT SKY PRESS
Box 416
Albany, Texas 76430

10   9   8   7   6   5   4   3   2   1

Library of Congress Cataloging-in-Publication Data

Boland, Irene, 1980–
    Wind the world over / by Irene Boland and Vanessa Kellogg.
        p. cm.
        ISBN 978-1-931721-94-3 (jacketed hardcover : alk. paper) 1. Wind power—
Juvenile literature—History. 2. Winds—Juvenile literature. I. Kellogg, Vanessa C.,
1977– II. Title.

    TJ823.B565 2007
    551.51'8—dc22   2007001339

Book and cover design by Isabel Lasater Hernandez
Edited by Cynthia Sellman Mendez
Printed in China through Asia Pacific Offset

WIND
the World Over

Irene Boland & Vanessa Kellogg

Illustrated by Tamberley Thomas

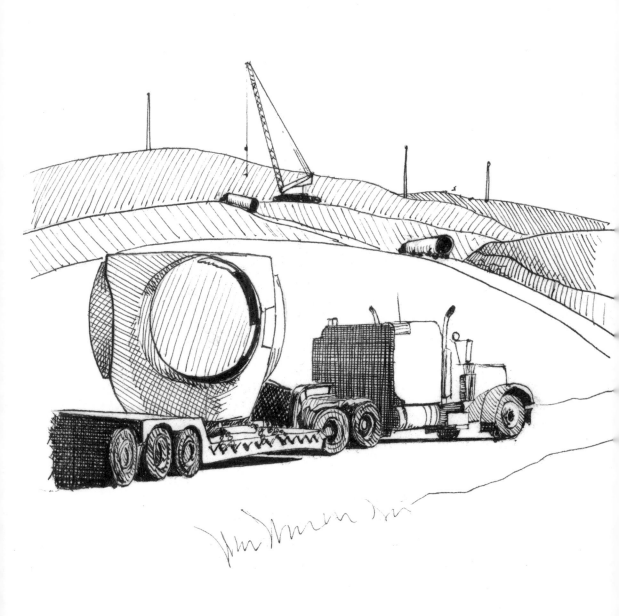

One hot Texas morning, Ruby woke up filled with excitement. "Wake up, Ian!" she nudged her brother. "It's a really big truck!"

Her red-headed brother's eyes popped open, and he pushed the curtains aside. "The wind turbines!" he cried. "Dad said they were coming soon!"

Together, they watched a parade of trucks carrying giant metal tubes big enough to drive a car through them.

"They are going to the wind farm up on Davis Ridge," Ruby said. "Look—here come the blades!" She pointed down the road. "Let's go climb the oak tree out front and watch them."

Ruby and Ian raced each other to the big oak tree in the front yard. They scrambled up the rope ladder to their favorite perches high in the tree. They watched as trucks drove by, loaded with tower sections, turbine blades, large coils of cable, and huge box-like parts called nacelles covering the gears and generators.

"Ruby, just look at those trucks!"

But Ruby wasn't listening to Ian. She had found a crumpled piece of yellow paper stuck between two of the branches.

"Hey! Somebody left us a note!"

Ruby unfolded the paper and read aloud: **You can't see me, but you know where I am.**

"Let me read." Ian peered at the paper in her hand. "Ruby, it's a riddle!"

Just then, the wind blasted through the tree's branches and whisked piles of orange and gold leaves into the air around them. When the leaves settled to the ground below, the children heard a woman whistling.

She was below them, walking by the tree. Behind her, stalks lay scattered about in the sand. It looked like they had fallen from the bundle she carried.

"Sand!?"

Ian hung upside down from the tree branch, his eyes round in amazement. "Ruby," he whispered, "This looks like a desert."

Ruby peered below.

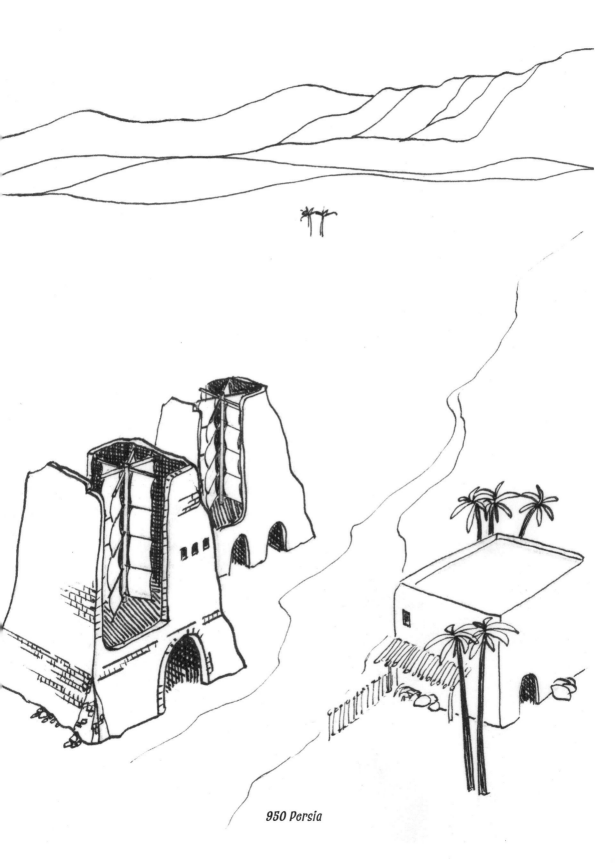

950 Persia

"What? How did we get here, Ian?"

They jumped down from the tree, picked up the fallen stalks, and followed the woman. She walked and walked, coming at last to a tall gate. It was made of stone and earth, and it had woven straw doors that spun in a circle.

"Excuse me," Ruby said to the woman. "What are you doing with these stalks?"

"I'm grinding barley with this windmill," she answered.

The woman placed the bundle of stalks over a bin and pulled hundreds of tiny seeds off the tips. The grain fell into the bin, slid through a chute and spilled into the eye of a large spinning stone disc. "The *baud* blows endlessly from June until October every year, turning the windmills around and around." Ruby wrote the word *baud* on her yellow piece of paper.

"In these months, we grind enough flour to feed fifteen families for the year," the woman said.

"Here, you dropped a couple," Ian said, holding out the stalks he had picked up under the tree.

"Thank you," said the Persian woman. "Would you like to have some breakfast with me?"

They followed their new friend inside a mud-brick house beside the tall mill. They sat together and ate oranges and pistachios, and delicious barley bread. Ruby asked about the *baud*.

The woman answered, "Here in Khorasan, the *baud* always blows from the mountains in the east and turns our windmills." She took Ruby's piece of paper and opened it. Then she wrote curvy lines on it. It was her language, Farsi.

She repeated, *"baud."*

Suddenly, a gust of wind blew open the door. Ian ran over to shut it, but he was stung by blowing sand. Outside, the thin trees bent with the wind. A crumpled piece of yellow paper skittered inside onto the floor.

"Look Ruby, another riddle!"

Ruby thanked the woman and followed him through the bright doorway.

"Hmmm," Ian said as he looked around. "Where are we?"

It was hilly, and in the distance, a man was flying a colorful kite high above a flooded grassy field.

"Ruby, listen to this," Ian said, reading from the paper: **I am always moving. If I stop, I will not exist.**

"Do you know what is always moving?" Ruby called to the Chinese kite flyer.

He shook his head. "It must be very tired," he grinned. Then he pointed across the field. "See how my windmill moves fast? The *feng* turns it around and around. The windmill pumps water from the Yangtze River to these rice paddies."

"What is *feng?*" Ruby asked.

"This is *feng!*" The kite-flyer motioned all around him with his arms opened wide.

The kids watched for a few minutes as he made the kite dance. Then he lowered the kite, and drew a picture on Ruby's paper.

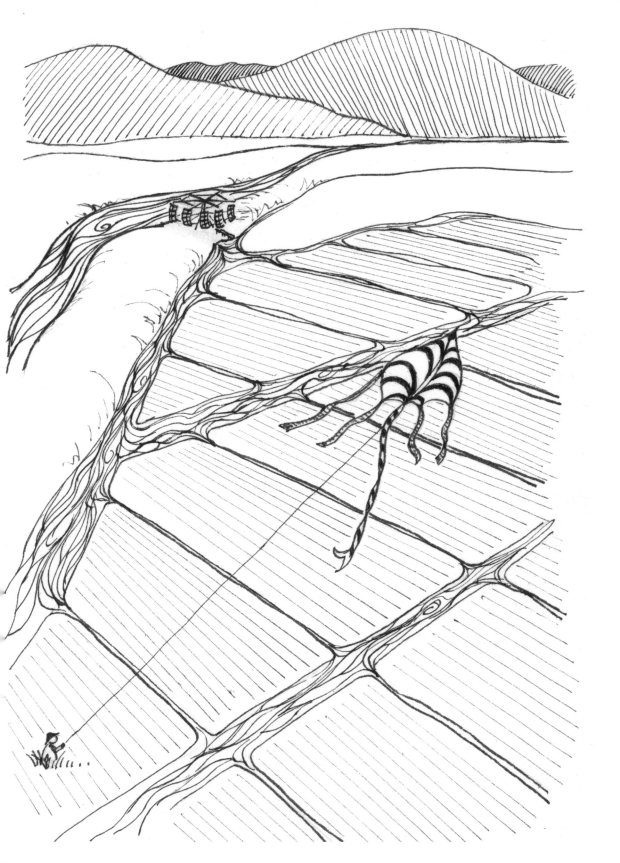

1200 China

"Feng?" asked Ruby.

"Yes, *feng,*" the man said grinning. "Now, would you like to taste some rice from this field?"

Ian and Ruby followed the man inside his house. They sat on a bamboo mat and used wooden chopsticks to eat sticky clumps of rice. When Ian finished and picked up his empty bowl, Ruby's eyes widened. On the table under his bowl was a folded piece of yellow paper. Ruby unfolded it and read aloud: **I come and go as I please.**

"Oh no, here we go again!" Ian said.

Ruby opened her mouth to ask the Chinese man about the riddle. But before she could, a gust of wind blew through the windows and carried puffs of white powder into the room. They heard a low grinding noise, and they started looking for the source of the sound. But billowing powder clouded the room cloaking everything in white. Ian and Ruby couldn't even see each other!

1350 The Netherlands

Ian sneezed, and Ruby patted her hands against the walls searching for the door. Even though they couldn't see anything at all, the grinding noise grew louder and louder.

"Where are we now?" Ruby asked through the clouds of powder.

Suddenly, the loud grinding noise became a high *screech* and then abruptly stopped. The whirls of powder fell slowly, like dry snow, and revealed a wooden machine. A door opened, and a man's wrinkled face and shoulders poked out.

"Hello! You're just in time to help me. C'mon!" He waved and disappeared.

Ruby and Ian walked toward the door and saw that they were at the top of a ladder. Down below, the man looked up at them. "Hurry now, we've already ground 40 sacks of rye flour today, but look, the Dutch *wind* has changed, and the windmill has stopped moving, so we will need to move my house."

He pointed up to the small flag, flapping in the wind, on top of the house.

"Move a house?" Ian asked. "He must be crazy!"

But Ruby was busy writing on her new paper, *wind,* noting that the man had pronounced the word *"veend."*

The sails of the windmill had indeed stopped turning. So Ian and Ruby scrambled down the ladder, and together they pushed and pushed as hard as they could on the windmill's tail pole. Slowly … slowly … the house began to turn. Finally, the windmill's giant sails caught the wind again, and the stocks began to spin high above them!

"Whew, now we can take a break." The miller sat down and wiped his forehead. Ruby decided to ask the man, "Sir, you said this is a Dutch *wind* blowing. Are we in the Netherlands?"

Just then, a bell rang inside the windmill, and the miller shook his head and ran up the ladder. "The hopper's empty—I have to refill it." He tossed them a small sack of flour. "Thank you for helping me move my windmill. And yes, this is the district of Holland in the Netherlands. Welcome to my town of Leiden!"

With a wave, he shut the door in a puff of flour.

Ruby and Ian lugged the sack of flour and found shade from the hot sun under a big rock.

"We're covered in flour!" Ruby said, brushing white dust off her arm.

"A-choo!" Ian replied.

"What are we going to do with this sack?" he asked. But Ruby did not answer. She had just noticed a yellow scrap in the pebbles on the ground.

"Ian, I can't believe it! It's another riddle!"

She read: **I am never hungry, but I help feed those who are.**

"I'm always hungry," Ian said.

"Where did you kids get flour in these old caves?"

They looked up and saw a woman in an apron. She was pointing behind them.

They turned and saw they were at the mouth of a dark cave.

The woman spoke again. "People lived in these caves in the cliffs above the river hundreds of years ago. Now everyone lives in the village over the hill. I'll show you how to get there, and we can take this flour to my bakery."

They followed the baker up the cliffs to see the village in the distance.

"Look!" proclaimed Ian. "It's a village with a windmill on every rooftop!"

"All these windmills grind grain into flour," the baker explained. "Many times more than the sack you are carrying. We use this flour to make delicious breads and pastries."

"Does the village eat that much bread?" Ian asked.

"No, we do not eat it all," the baker laughed. "We take much of the flour we mill to sell in Paris. We have *grand vent* here in Saumur, France. Some days the *vent* keeps our mills grinding day and night."

They arrived at a cart full of large sacks of flour.

"Hop in! You can help me deliver this flour to Paris," said the baker.

Ian and Ruby climbed into the cart behind the baker's horse and sat on the rough sacks. Ruby scribbled the word *vent* on her paper. The baker gave them a loaf of bread to share as the cart clattered down the road. They listened to

1790 France

the wheels turning around and around, and soon they grew very tired.

They drifted off to sleep.

When Ruby opened her eyes, the cart was gone. She was lying next to Ian in tall grass.

"How long have I been asleep?" she wondered, watching purple and pink clouds drift across the low, late afternoon sun.

She started to wake Ian, but noticed a yellow piece of paper in his hand, where he had been holding the bread. Ruby slipped the paper from her brother's grasp and opened it as he rubbed his eyes.

"Listen, Ian! It's another riddle!"

But Ian was busy staring at the cow munching grass noisily right beside him.

Ruby read: **I dry things out, but I bring water, too.**

"I'm thirsty." Ian groaned. "Where are we? Where did all these cows come from?"

"I hear water!" Ruby pointed toward a tall windmill. It was one tower with a large metal pinwheel of blades. The

1930 United States

blades were spinning a squeaky *eeeh-aigh eeeh-aigh* as they moved around and around. "Ian, I think it's a drinking fountain for the cows," she said.

At the base, a slow trickle poured into a large basin, where several cows were drinking.

"That's right! These are all my thirsty cattle."

The kids jumped up to see a man on a horse. "It hasn't rained here for weeks," he said. "But with this windmill, even when everything is bone-dry, we can we still get water. See, when the wind blows, it pumps water from a well deep in the ground and fills up the trough. We just have to add a little oil to the gears every once in a while to keep 'er moving."

"Are you going to climb this windmill?" Ian asked, remembering the Dutch windmill. "We can help you turn it!"

The cowboy grinned. "Well, I don't need to turn it. See? It has a wind vane in the back so it can point itself into the wind. But I do need to oil it, and I'm not so keen on climbing, myself. Are you good climbers?"

"Yes!" they cried, thinking of their favorite tree.

"Be careful," the cowboy said, handing them the spouted oil can.

Ian and Ruby climbed to the top of the tower together, and Ruby tipped the little spout to coat the moving gears.

"I thank you kindly for your help," said the man. "Let's have a drink of water underneath this shade tree." The cowboy handed them his canteen. "So, how did you two end up here on Davis Ridge?"

"Davis Ridge!" Ruby and Ian looked at each other. "We live just over that hill," Ruby explained and pointed.

The cowboy chuckled, "Oh, all right then. I didn't know anyone lived over there, but y'all had best be gettin' on home before sunset. I'm going to check on another windmill at our next camp a couple miles from here."

Ian and Ruby waved good-bye and headed uphill toward their home. At the top of the hill, they saw a small oak tree that looked familiar, but no house. They tried to climb the small tree, but only the lowest branch was big enough to hold them.

"Ruby, how are we going to get home?" Ian asked.

But Ruby didn't know. They huddled together on the low branch as the wind howled through the tree and the last ray of the Texas sun disappeared behind Davis Ridge.

It was almost completely dark when a familiar light twinkled. It was their front porch light!

"Dinner time!" yelled Mom. They were back home in their favorite tree.

Ruby and Ian shimmied down the rope ladder just as their father walked up the sidewalk.

"Dad, will the new wind farm give us food for our dinner?" Ian asked, pointing to the ridge where several towers had been built that day.

"It's not a farm with animals and vegetables, Ian. This wind farm will create electricity that can provide power not just to our house, but to several towns here in Texas."

Then he thought for a minute. "Actually, we use electricity to heat our coffee pot, bake our lasagna, and freeze our ice cream ..." Dad looked at Ian and Ruby. "So, I guess you're right. The wind farm will help us cook and store our food. I never thought about it that way."

Ruby looked up. "But Dad, hasn't wind always been used for free power?"

"That's true, Ruby. Wind is a powerful source of energy, and we don't have to pay for it. We also don't have to burn fuel to make electricity, and that helps make the air cleaner to breathe."

He stopped for a second and looked at the children again. "How did you know that?"

Ruby and Ian just grinned. "Oh, we read it somewhere," they replied, keeping their grins.

After dinner, Ruby emptied her pockets of the scraps of yellow paper she had collected through the day. She pinned each piece onto the big map of the world next to their bunk beds. She could read the riddles all together now.

You can't see me, but you know where I am.

I am always moving. If I stop, I will not exist.

I come and go as I please.

I am never hungry, but I help feed those who are.

I dry things out, but I bring water, too.

"I've got it!" exclaimed Ruby. "The answer to each of the riddles is WIND!"

"You're right!" cried Ian excitedly. "Wind is invisible, but you know where it is because you can see what it moves. But if it stops, the wind is gone. And it can go anywhere it wants—you can't make it blow."

"Yeah!" Ruby said. "It also helps feed hungry people by turning windmills that grind grains for food. And the wind can dry out land, but it also can pump water out of the ground."

"Wow." Ian said. "Wind power can do so many things, and it has a different name in every land!"

baud—باد

feng—風

veend—wind

vent

wind

Glossary

Bamboo—(a) Any of various usually woody, temperate or tropical grasses of the genera Arundinaria, Bambusa, Dendrocalamus, Phyllostachys, or Sasa. Certain species of bamboo can reach heights of from 20 to 30 meters (66 to 98 feet); (b) the hard or woody, jointed, often hollow stems of these plants, used in construction, crafts, and fishing poles

Barley—(a) a widely distributed cereal plant belonging to the genus Hordeum, of the grass family, having awned flowers that grow in tightly bunched spikes, with three small additional spikes at each node; (b) the grain of such plant

Baud—the word for "wind" in Farsi

Cable—an insulated electrical conductor, often in strands, or a combination of electrical conductors insulated from one another

Dutch—something or someone from The Netherlands, also called Holland

Electricity [H]—The energy of moving electrons, the current of which is used as a source of power

Environment [H]—All the natural and living things around us; the earth, air, weather, plants, and animals all make up our environment

Farsi—the modern Iranian language of Iran and western Afghanistan, written in the Arabic alphabet; modern Persian.

Feng—the word for "wind" in Chinese

Gear—(a) part, as a disk, wheel, or section of a shaft, having cut teeth of such form, size, and spacing that they mesh with teeth in another part to transmit or receive force and motion; (b) an assembly of such parts

Generator—a machine that converts one form of energy into another, especially mechanical energy into electrical energy

Grand vent—the words for "heavy wind" in French

Khorasan [F]—Khorasan is situated in the East of Iran, is the "place where the sun rises". Historical Khorasan, also known as "Great Khorasan" included present day Khorasan as well as Transoxiana and Afghanistan

Leiden [L]—A city and municipality in the province of South Holland in The Netherlands

Miller—a person who owns or operates a mill, especially a mill that grinds grain into flour

Nacelle [H]—the cover for the gearbox, drive train, and generator of a wind turbine

Persian—something or someone from Persia, the name for the land that is now Iran

Renewable energy [H]—sometimes also referred to as "alternative energy," "clean power," or "green power," renewable energy is energy derived from resources that are regenerative or that cannot be depleted. Types of renewable energy resources include wind, solar, biomass, geothermal, and moving water

Rice paddy—an irrigated or flooded field where rice is grown

Saumur [FRA]—Saumur is a town and commune in the Maine-et-Loire département, or county, of France on the Loire River

Tail pole [DW]—a long pole extending from the Dutch windmill, passing between two rungs of the ladder and then curving slightly downward, with its end is firmly fastened to the end of the ladder by means of two upright oaken posts; it is used both to turn the windmill and to help take the pressure of the wind on the sails and the mill body

Turbine blade—a large aerodynamic arm of a wind turbine that turns as the wind blows; there are typically three blades on modern wind turbines

Vent—the word for "wind" in French

Wind [H]—Moving air caused by the sun's heat, the earth, and the oceans, forcing air to rise and fall in cycles

Wind farm [H]—a piece of land on which wind turbines are sited for the purpose of electricity generation

Windmill—any of various machines for grinding, pumping, etc., driven by the force of the wind acting upon a number of vanes or sails

Wind turbine [H]—also known as a wind generator, a wind turbine is a modern day machine used to convert wind energy into electricity

Wind vane—a device, as a rod to which a freely rotating pointer is attached, for indicating the direction of the wind.

Wind power [H]—Another term for "wind energy," wind power is power generated by converting the mechanical energy of the wind into electrical energy through the use of a wind generator

Yangtze River [CGEE]—the longest river in Asia and third longest in the world [flowing] generally south through Sichuan into Yuanan then northeast and east across central China through Sichuan, Hubei, Auhui, and Juangsu provinces to its mouth, 3,720 miles, in the East China Sea north of Shanghai

[AHD] American Heritage Dictionary online: www.dictionary.com

[D] On-line Dictionary: http://www.dictionary.com

[H] Horizon Wind Energy website: http://www.horizonwind.com/about/ftkc/glossary.aspx

[F] Farsi Net: http://www.farsinet.com/mashhad/khorasan.html

[L] Leiden Stadsportal: http://stadsportal.leiden.nl/stadsportaal/home.do

[FRA] Jolivot, Nicolas. Saumurois des moulins & des meuniers : heurs et malheurs de la meunerie aì vent. Paul Keruel et Jen-Louis Giard Editions de L' Anjou. June 1994. Digne-les-Bains./ Nicolas Jolivot.

[DW] The Dutch Windmill by Frederick Stokhuyzen, found at http://www.nt.ntnu.no/users/haugwarb/DropBox/The%20Dutch%20Windmill%20Stokhuyzen%201962.htm

[CGEE] The Yangtze River: http://cgee.hamline.edu/rivers/Resources/river_profiles/Yangtze.html

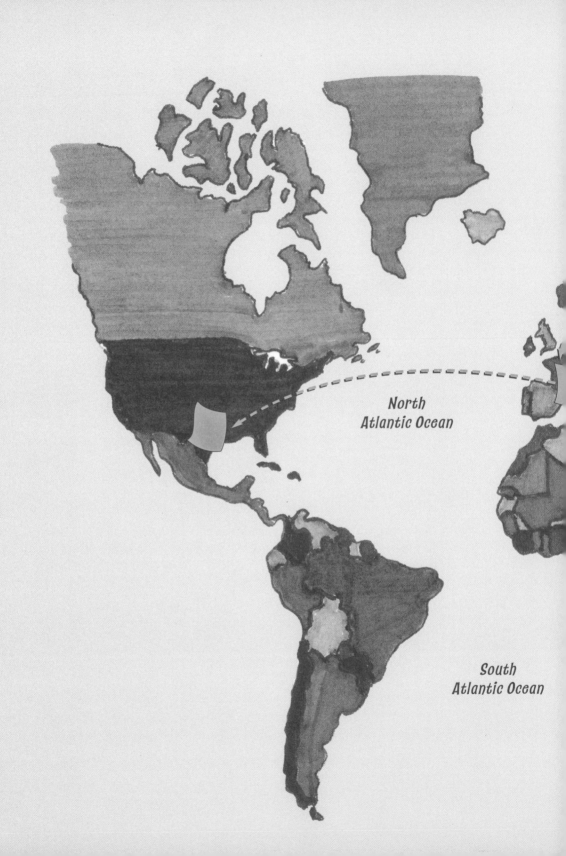

North
Atlantic Ocean

South
Atlantic Ocean